Attack Your Fears with Concentration and a Positive Attitude

by

Joshua Magloire

authorHOUSE™

1663 LIBERTY DRIVE, SUITE 200
BLOOMINGTON, INDIANA 47403
(800) 839-8640
WWW.AUTHORHOUSE.COM

First published by AuthorHouse 05/05/05

ISBN: 1-4208-0825-7 (sc)

Printed in the United States of America
Bloomington, Indiana

This book is printed on acid-free paper.

DEDICATION

This book is dedicated to my grand mother Bessie Magloire

Table of Contents

INTRODUCTION

One morning at the office, my friend Ronnie asked me to explain to him the meaning of life with two other guys looking and waiting to hear my answer. I was caught off guard because I could not respond. I didn't know what to say. I went home thought about it and gave him an answer the next day and at the same time thought this was a good idea for the introduction to my next book.

Life, I explain is about learning, that is why we must go through different experiences; the good and so called bad experiences. They are all important in teaching us valuable lessons, lessons, when learned well make our lives easier and easier as time goes by.

When you have learned something you understand it and you are now free to make wise decisions.

Freedom comes with understanding, freedom to live your life the way you choose to. Let's say you suffer from headaches regularly and every time you take an aspirin to relieve the pain. You can keep doing this or try to understand the cause of the problem. Maybe, according to health professionals, you have a stomach problem due to lack of cleansing or you have some emotional situation like refusing to forgive someone for the wrongs they have done to you or you are angry at your parents for the way they have treated you, compared to your siblings. Maybe you just have an anger problem. By understanding the cause, you can take the necessary steps to free yourself from the headache totally.

I always tell the people around me, who are going through relationship and other types of problems, to learn the lesson that the situation has to offer. You must learn the lesson, if not you will be taking a hit for nothing, as a famous rapper once said. A real tragedy in life is not learning the lesson from which a certain experience was intended.

THE IMPORTANCE OF NERVOUSNESS

I spent much of my younger days fighting the feelings of nervousness. I really hated the feelings, the sensations, the pounding heart, accelerated breathing, especially when I had to face an audience. I don't know when and where it started, but that was going to be my big challenge in life. Everybody experiences nervousness when addressing an audience or doing anything else for the first time but somehow I viewed it differently and had a hard time for a while. I guess that was one of the roads I had to travel in life so I could eventually write this book. We all lose our balance in one way or another at some time in our lives and it is our jobs to get back on track.

I have read many books over the years and I have tried nine hundred and ninety nine techniques to finally get rid of this problem; so I thought. It turns out that I have been fighting something that is absolutely natural. It is the way we were designed. That's exactly how nature intended it to be. In other words if you never get nervous you are not normal. The big challenge is getting use to the feelings. One way of doing that is by reminding yourself to do, at least one courageous act daily.

Nervousness is your mind and body generating the right amount of energy to do the task at hand. When you are nervous your pulse rate and your breathing increase. That means the flow of blood increases, requiring much more oxygen, which is needed in generating the required energy. Don't be frightened, it's just your body demanding a greater supply of oxygen at that particular moment. Allow it to breath freely instead of trying to suppress or control the process. Breathe with your mouth while you talk. That will enable you to supply your body with the extra air it needs and be able to talk at the same time without distraction or interruption. You may also experience other sensations in your body which are also part of the process of conditioning you for that particular task.

It is important to understand nervousness because it can become a major distraction in your life. Nervousness is good for us, its important in helping us get through our daily lives with all the energy and drive we need. The problem too many of us face is being frightened by the process. Heart pounding, intense breathing, electrical sensation running through the muscles is enough to send a person running. Every where you look there is someone staying away from a person, place or thing because of the uncomfortable feelings associated with it.

The chemical adrenaline is responsible for the phenomenon called nervousness. When you are faced with a situation, your body will release the right amount of adrenaline necessary to get the job done and it is always right on tract.

The problem begins when you become frightened by the initial nervous sensations going on in your body. That is where you experience the irrational thinking of danger and humiliation. This frightened reaction causes the release of too much of this chemical into the blood streams resulting in profuse sweating, trembling, weakness in the knees and countless other reactions people experience. So the problem isn't nervousness, it is a lack of understanding of our selves and the way we function.

Adrenaline to us is like what gas is to a car. The car needs more energy or power to move off than when it's just idling in one place. When it is climbing a hill with or without a heavy load or just cruising along a flat stretch, a different amount of energy is needed in each case.

You are walking down the side walk and you realize an out of control car is heading directly at you. There is a vast difference in the amount of energy the body will generate in both cases, one being just walking and the next, having to fight for your life. Get use to the way the body generates its energy.

You can now go on your daily lives being ready to welcome the feeling of nervousness whenever it shows up. It is always going to be there because it is a part of your makeup. In the past it was once viewed as a weakness, now you know it as your source of power.

THE BENEFITS OF CONCENTRATION

Concentration is one of the most important skills any man can learn in his life time. You become more creative and more productive in what ever you do. Your mind is more at peace and your energy level increases. Your confidence in yourself and your abilities also improve. When you concentrate you bring all your energies together to accomplish a specific task. Now what was considered difficult is now easily handled.

To concentrate you have to be absolutely clear about what you need to do and how you want to do it. If you can describe your goal in one clear sentence, a phrase or even one word, you are well on your way to good concentration. The repetition of these words keeps you forever focused.

All my life, I have always heard that a man can always accomplish anything he wants if he keeps at it. There is enough energy in any one of us to achieve our desires no matter what they may be. When this energy is focused or concentrated we can blow away any obstacle in our paths.

When you are distracted, your attention moves from one place to the next. You experience fragmentation meaning your attention is broken up. This explains why its midday and you haven't done quarter of the work you normally complete easily by nine o'clock. When your attention is fragmented, you lack energy and you will not be effective at anything you do until you get it together.

As your concentration skills improve, 'self consciousness' has less of an effect on you. The self conscious person makes mistakes because he is not concentrating fully and that leads to self criticism which then leads to self hate. The longer he stays in this phase the worst things get. Self hate is a low estimate of one's self, better known as low self esteem. A person with low self esteem definitely experiences inferiority complex, the feeling that others are better than you. That trend sets one on a downward spiral to a life of hell where things only get worst.

A person experiencing inferiority complex, low self esteem suffers from a feeling of inadequacy and vulnerability and feels unworthy. She is very negative and doesn't think that she could achieve anything worthwhile. In fact she feels undeserving of anything good. Her vulnerability also makes her very aggressive, an attempt to stay free from danger. In fact she uses anger to keep people from hurting her. It's her best defensive mechanism.

I said to this lady one time, the only reason you get angry so easily and so often is because you are just protecting you self; she agreed with me. That's the way human and animals attempt to stay clear from danger.

Jealousy is a feeling of inadequacy where the individual feels that he is unable to accomplish what his peers already have. This is not natural and it doesn't feel right. Held for too long, that unhealthy feeling gets worst and he begins to resent his more successful brother, because he is constantly reminded of those feelings which by now has become painful. Jealousy gone unchecked, leads to resentment of another's success which is referred to as envy. That pattern of thinking leads to hate and this is a dangerous situation for any body to be in. A man will hate you if you remind him of something painful about himself.

Very successful people have enemies whose desires are to send them crashing to the ground. On your way up to the top everybody identifies with you, because everyone wants to better his or her life. You get all the love and support you need to get there. You quickly realize there are only few people at the top. Now, the same ones who cheered you on your way up want you back down simply because you are a reminder of where they are; a place they don't necessarily like. That's where the attempts to destroy you begin.

The guilt ridden man doesn't feel worthy of any thing good. He feels that he has done something bad

9

and should be punished. People with low self esteem will suffer from this emotion more than others. This is one of the reasons why some become compulsive gamblers. They almost always lose everything because of the need to lose.

Some parents are experts at making their children feel guilt and wonder why these people are not very successful. The way we were conditioned is you cannot be rewarded for doing something wrong. So while you may use guilt for you own personal reasons, you are preventing your victims from developing into full grown, successful, happy productive people.

Worry and anxiety are feelings of inadequacy where you expect the worst to befall you. People with high self esteem constantly pep themselves up with positive self talk on a daily basis while those with low self esteem do the exact opposite. In fact inferiority complex and feelings of inadequacy are caused by constant affirmation of negative self talk which takes you further and further into a state of hell.

When you have succeeded in making a person self conscious you have literally started them on a downward spiral to a life of endless difficulties. This kid spends all his adult life being fat because his relatives didn't let a day pass without reminding him of his large frame. Within a short time he was fully convinced that this is how he was meant to be. And as we all know, a man is compelled to experience his deep beliefs as long as he keeps entertaining those thoughts.

It is comforting to know that at any time we can turn our situations around by choosing for our selves a way of thinking that is in tune with the type of lives we want to live.

SET GOALS

Many people oppose the idea of setting goals thinking it never works for them. I can understand the need for spontaneity as far as having fun is concerned but you need to set life goals. You are in your thirties, how many houses would you like to own by age forty? How much money would you like to have invested? Would a college degree help you get a better position at your work place? Approximately how many kids do you want and what type of person do you want for a mate? If you don't have goals, these things may or may never come, but if you write out a good plan, you will be at or close to your mark. Like they say, if you shoot for the moon and miss, you will be among the stars.

I notice, people who don't have clear specific goals, tend to watch too much television and talk too long on the phone to friends who are of no help. They are not paying attention to the negative influences around them. They spend precious time around negative people who literally drag them down. When you have a clear specific goal and a good plan, you will naturally have little tolerance for anything that hinders your progress.

Do you notice how effective you are in utilizing your time in getting things done when you have a job to go to as opposed to having nowhere to go or nothing specific to do? You wake up in the morning and have x amount of time to get prepared in order to get to work on time and that requires focus. While at work, you are planning the rest of the day so no time is wasted. You allocate a certain amount of time for every other activity, even the number of hours you will sleep before work the next day. That type of concentration keeps you healthy and productive because you are setting and accomplishing many goals on a daily basis.

UNDERSTANDING FEAR

Fear is a false emotion that debilitates and incapacitates. It is a manufactured man made emotion, meaning, it's not real. The fear you experience is like a plastic snake to a person who is petrified of snakes; its an illusion. We create this emotion due to our own bad experience or as a result of stories told to us of the experiences of others. For example some people who were in the World Trade Center at the time of the tragedy will keep away from tall buildings for years to come no matter what. Some who have never been in a sky scraper before will never get into one because of the mental images they have created of the dangers of being in that type of building.

The best way to free yourself from your fears is, understanding the real problem by noticing carefully your reaction to the situation. Since it's an illusion, you must make up your mind to do the thing feared, using concentration and a positive attitude. By a positive attitude I mean getting the job done no matter how hard or how long it takes.

Once you have reached that state of mind in accomplishing anything, getting there is usually faster and easier than expected. We all know that there is little that could stand in the way of a truly determined person.

You are an adult and you will not go near a pool because of a bad childhood experience where you almost drowned. Whenever the thought of swimming comes up what do you immediately think of? Do you see your self drowning, other horrible things happening? This image in your mind is what you have been reacting to all along; that's the real problem. So now you know the exact problem you can now concentrate on the exact opposite. See yourself swimming like an expert or doing what ever you want to do and being successful at it.

Be very specific about what you want to do in the water. Maybe you want to be a life guard or you just want to swim for fun, or maybe you live close to the beach and want to be able to protect your family incase someone is in danger. To be successful you need to find your point of concentration.

Now that you are absolutely clear about what you want to do, you can move on to the next step. If I were you I would pray for the 'courage' to do that particular thing followed by an affirmation. An example of an affirmation is I now have enough courage to be a fantastic swimmer.

The next step is, understanding that the fear sensation you feel when doing something that prevents you from enjoying a normal life is in fact good for you, it is there to empower you. The nervous feelings are helping you get ready for that particular situation. So go ahead and do the thing feared with that mentality.

You will experience a little more freedom everyday; freedom to be the way you want to be.

The right name for these strange feelings we experience in our bodies that we call nervousness is ADRENALINE RUSH because that's exactly what it is, and not fear as we previously thought.

I used water to explain my point but the idea can be applied to any area of your life.

To reiterate the steps:

1. Notice your thought pattern when you think about doing the thing feared.

2. Think the opposite

3. Find your point of concentration; be clear about what you want to do.

4. Pray for courage to do that particular thing

5. Repeat a positive affirmation of courage

6. Know that what you call nervousness is really an ADRENALINE RUSH where the body

generates the right amount of power to do the task at hand.

FEAR IN DISGUISE

We must understand that fear has many different faces. In other words, it shows up in different disguises. The main purpose of fear is to prevent you from living a normal healthy productive life. It stands in the way of you dreams and desires and keeps success away.

Anger is one of the children of fear because it acts as a block. While some anger is actually good for you, too much is very unhealthy. It's something we all know from experience.

Worry, anxiety, jealousy, hate, resentment, criticism and all other negative behaviors are the children of fear because they have the same mind clogging effect.

Let's look at criticism and see what it's all about. Very critical people are afraid of being hurt. In fact they hurt very easily. They are easily affected by what you say and how you treat them. This is why John spends so much energy trying to divert your attention away from him to the other person. Notice how hurt he feels or how angry he gets when you give him a taste of his own medicine.

Anthony hates you but cannot reveal the real reason why he does because that's too personal. If he does, he would be showing his weakness, so instead he makes one up. And he shows fear when he continuously attacks you, verbally and or physically especially when unprovoked.

I know that we all experience these emotions at one time or another and that's all right because we are humans. The problem starts for you, when these emotions intensify over time.

THE BASIC CONCEPT OF LIFE

Life is all about giving and receiving, where it is necessary to focus mainly on giving. It is not better to give than to receive because they are two important aspects of our lives.

What you get in life is almost always based on what you give. Lets look at a musician who puts all his attention on giving his audience high quality music and is very concerned about satisfying them. He is finally able to accomplish that goal and reaps the benefits which are endless. First, his records sell very quickly and he always has sold out shows. The inflow of money at that point is tremendous. The love he gets from the fans is overwhelming, and the state of being an accomplished musician is the most wonderful feeling. The mere act of playing music to the people is an incredible feeling in itself. So this is how much a musician benefits if he just keeps his attention on giving the best that he possibly can.

You are the owner of a restaurant and your main concern is satisfying your customers, which is what it should be all about. The easy way to do that is to have a pleasant staff serve tasty food at a reasonable price. This doesn't take a whole lot of effort and it only takes a few extra dollars and a few more minutes to make your food tastier. If that's your determination, you may soon have to expand because of customer turnout. We always get so much more in return when we focus mainly on giving.

In all other areas of life, your giving should be done intelligently. There are people who will quickly make you their chauffer, butler or slave long before you even realize what's going on. Be nice to some people once and you are their servant for life. That type of giving is silly and should be stopped whenever you choose to.

You should not allow anyone to distract you from giving, because it's the way you receive your blessings in life. You treat your mate very well, but she has a low estimate of herself, causing her to deliberately do things to hurt you. This is not your problem it's hers because she feels unworthy of your good. All you have to do is move on to someone else who will appreciate you a little more.

Although you must focus mainly on giving, there is definitely a problem if nothing is coming in. There should be a flow, which means energy going out and energy coming in. You can recognize a one sided relationship easily because it just doesn't feel natural. Your friend Elsa in New Jersey is happy to talk to you any time as long as the call is on you. Now a relationship like this fades away quickly. What about the husband who takes advantage of his sweet wife by having her, take care of all the bills on her own year in year out?

I have always found it difficult accepting truly selfish people as my good friends and associates. They represent a block, in some way they are clogged up mentally. It's a form of sickness and it doesn't feel right being close friends. I don't dislike these individuals it just feels better keeping my distance.

The greedy man spoils everything. He is not necessarily a bad person, his thinking is not right. The problem with this individual is he concentrates on money and wealth to the point where he becomes desensitized to everything else around him. He will do away with his own family if they get between him and his money; that's how bad things can get. As far as he is concerned, the company, the employees and there future can perish, as long as he get his cut.

He appears to have a one tract mind. He is trying to find peace doing what gives him the exact opposite. He becomes more and more desperate because he keeps coming up empty; empty inside. The wallet is filled but he is just not happy.

The good feelings come when your life is balanced. A balanced life has two sides; a going and a coming; an inflow and an out flow; a giving and a receiving. The problem begins when there is too much of one and too little of the other. The greedy is all about taking and grabbing that's why he can never be satisfied.

LOVE TO GET LOVE

Many complain about not getting enough love; young and old. To have anything in life you must do something for it even if it means just thinking about it. Start with your immediate family. Give them a little more attention than you normally do and show some genuine interest. That gesture is free and effortless and they will surely appreciate it. You will begin to notice how they treat you differently and you will love it too.

There is no need for an adult to blame his criminal actions on a lack of love growing up. We have seen it time and time again, people blaming their terrible actions on no one being around to love them.

Love is very important in maintaining our balance, but you should not sit around and wait for it no matter how young you are. It is something that comes to you in proportion to how much you give. So if you complain about not getting any you should blame your self equally for not giving enough.

ARE YOU LIVING JUST FOR YOU?

I know many people who see absolutely no problem with doing just enough for themselves and their immediate families. How many people do you know would build or buy a house with others in mind, example having a guess room that would make a visitor and everybody else feel comfortable?

You set up your house to accommodate only your family, then your nosey uncle Loui comes to town and must stay at your place for a month. That's a month of discomfort. First the bed rooms are too close and not enough bathrooms. So here is this man being too close for comfort minding your business and to make it worse he thinks it's his right to do as he pleases like spending whatever amount of time he wants in your single bathroom.

I cannot live with the idea of doing just enough for me. Can you imagine your half brother being sick and you just cannot come up with the thirty thousand needed to save his life? This could be a painful situation which can be avoided by having a different mind set.

If you focus on having enough and extra incase others are desperately in need, maybe you will end up having in abundance. When you expect more that's what you may end up having.

You benefit 'big time' when you look out for others. If you have been thinking that you could get along with a few thousand dollars in your account, your mind will now be focused on tens of thousands even hundreds of thousands. And if one million was just right for you, now you want a lot more. The paradox is you are actually making yourself wealthier. So the trick to prosperity is putting others first.

THE SUCCESSFUL MANAGER

A good manager has one major goal as far as his job is concerned and that is to satisfy his customers. The way he goes about this depends on his understanding of the human nature. Everybody wants to feel important, they crave for it. People patronize your business because of what you have to offer and the way they are treated. The customer needs to feel that you care for him or he will go some place else if he has a choice. The good news about this is meeting those requirements are not difficult at all.

A good manager's skills lie in his ability to get his coworkers to give at least a hundred percent everytime.

He understands that he will never accomplish that goal if he goes around bossing and bullying people around. He has to be strict about the work to be done while at the same time showing respect and treating everybody like equals.

People will resent you when you try to make them feel inferior simply because it doesn't feel right. That resentment in the workplace is what creates fragmentation. So instead of working like one big machine, the work force is broken up mentally at least. At this point, even the best workers can't give their best. Their energy level is too low. We all know there is little to nothing a broken up thing can accomplish.

Almost every manager I have encountered doesn't seem to understand what the job is all about. Most of them are egotistical self centered individuals who almost always screw things up. Its about how fast you obey his command, your tone of voice when you talk to him, how you chose to address her, Jenny, Miss Tillett or Mrs. Tillett and all unnecessary crap that has absolutely nothing to do with the success of the company. Their ignorance makes them liabilities.

Anthony Lizette and Dave are three of my associates who hold managerial positions. These three are convinced that their positions make them superior to the other workers and they practice that mentality when ever an opportunity shows up. They will make up an excuse if they have to, to satisfy their selfish egotistical needs by willfully insulting and disrespecting a fellow employee. Because it's their right, according to their beliefs, you should not even try to respond because you will be written up or disciplined. This is the perfect recipe for destroying or at least damaging a company.

You come in to work today with the intention of getting even with this idiot who just refuses to learn how to talk to people in the right way. With that frame of mind you cannot give your best even if you want to.

Many businesses have gone belly up in record time because of ignorant staff and or management who don't understand what their jobs entail. I remember listening to a New York radio station and thought to my self, this company is not going to last. I got a sense of the nature of the relationship between the hosts one morning while I was listening and it wasn't right. You cannot have a poor relationship with others in any setting and expect to flourish at the same time. I can't remember exactly when the station went off the air, but it was a very short time after; more like a few weeks to a couple of months; no longer.

KEEP IT SIMPLE

That's my motto in life because it works well for me. Simple is always better because the opposite of this is complicated.

Have you ever tried having two or three serious relationships at once? I am a big flirt but that's about it. Can you imagine what it feels like being at home with your mate and almost having a heart attack everytime the phone rings, fearing it might be Marleen calling to find out why you haven't called her in two weeks? Well I have thought about it and I don't like the idea.

The Jack of all trade might just be a little confused personality. I understand you may be talented, but if one minute you are fixing this car for your neighbor for a fee and the next minute you are doing electrical work for your brother because your price is cheaper and four other forms of employment simultaneously, it is time for you to adopt the mentality, 'KEEP IT SIMPLE'. Figure out that one thing that you truly love and master it to the best of your ability and do other things if you have the time and are feeling up to it.

Many times in our lives we find ourselves in complicated situations and must come up with a simple solution. You are a very beautiful lady and you have a man whom you love very much but other men are after you like flies, just wear an engagement ring even if you are not. That should simplify things unless you enjoy the attention.

Most of the foods that we eat, carbohydrates, proteins and other minerals are in their complex states at the time of ingestion. The chewing and all the other chemical reactions that take place are to break them down to their simplest forms. That's the only way they could be absorbed into the blood streams and be used by the body. That's a good example for simplifying every day situations.

It's our jobs to take complicated things and simplify them and not the other way around like so many do. Example, in order to work effectively at the workshop it would be a good idea to have all the tools and every thing else in their right places. With enough space and comfort the worker is more effective and productive.

Many businesses fail when things become too complicated. I often say to the people at my present job, you know the nature of the work and what is required. Come in and get it done to the best of your abilities and go home to your other life; simple as that.

Most of us have jobs that are supposed to be quite simple but the twisted personalities, be it managers or coworkers are going to make it one of the most difficult tasks you ever perform. We can all relate to this statement very well. Your task is simple beyond belief and you are good at it too, but at the end of the day you are exhausted and frustrated and would rather not go in the next day. That's mainly due to the employees making their personalities and all their problems a part of the job.

The 'keep it simple' mentality can be very important if you are in a situation where your life is potentially in danger. This is not the time and place for complicated thinking. You need one clear goal; something to concentrate on. See yourself at home in time for dinner with your family. See the face of a loved one who is counting on you. You fell in the icy water and you are in danger of freezing to death, see your self at home in your room and on your bed wrapped in a warm comforter. That type of concentration keeps your head clear enabling to do the right things necessary for your survival.

WHAT GOES AROUND COMES AROUND

This saying is as literal as the food you eat. If it is good it will nourish your body and if it is bad it could hurt you. Like electricity, you can't see it, but it's very real.

Everything is energy and what you say or do to people, the money clothing and all the material things you give to others are all energy. The nature of energy is to move constantly which means that there must be an inflow and an out flow, a going and a coming; something we all experience in our lives.

People are usually surprised when that energy comes around to them. In many cases they don't even understand what's happening. That greedy Aunt of yours is so surprised that you are not sharing your wealth with her the way she thinks you should. This man I know has lost everything in his late forties and it seems that every one but he knows for a fact it's because of his nasty, selfish behavior.

Many people get a position of power and focus their attention on using and abusing others. This is a regular human behavior in every walk of life; so it seems. We see over and over again people rising to the top then ill treating their fellow men and soon after falling right on their backs. This happens all the time, it's unfortunate how so many are not paying more attention to this problem.

I have seen and heard people fall from grace so many times I am forced to pay attention to how others should be treated. That I know plays a huge role in my success in life. I cannot afford to work so hard for so long, finally get to where I want to be, then engage in ignorant behaviors that could quickly take me right back to my struggles. After all these sacrifices you have made, you want to enjoy all the good things life has to offer for as long as possible.

Many people never get back on their feet because they don't understand how they fell in the first place. Like some drug addicts, many would deny the fact that they need an attitude adjustment.

THE POWER OF A WOMAN

A woman has tremendous influence over her mate. The lady, who is going to be at your side for the next few years or even the rest of your life, has the power to make or break you. She can have control of your mental, physical and financial state and be very good at it without much effort. With love and support from his wife, a broke man can become very successful in record time.

The lady who constantly opposes and fights her man weakens him. Over time he looses his creativity, effectiveness and ability to prosper. You just have to look around, notice couples and see for yourself.

Looking back, I am happy that I met my x girlfriend but at the time, I knew we were not going to accomplish anything worthwhile if we kept fighting each other. In fact I reminded her constantly that couples cannot succeed at anything if there is no peace in the relationship. She finally agreed with me.

A woman with extremely low self esteem will take you to the land of poverty and keep you there until you get back to your senses and make some changes. She doesn't feel worthy of any good and mentally blocks herself and everyone else around her from any kind of success.

EVERY BODY WANTS TO FEEL IMPORTANT

The best way to give is to make people feel important. If someone needs food clothing and shelter, then you should do your best in helping that individual. While it is good to give in that way, your best giving is non material, it's free. Showing Timmy how to make his own money and be his own man is much better than giving him ten dollars everytime you see him.

When you make a person feel important, you make that person like himself more and that increases his self worth. In other words his self esteem increases which improves his self confidence. At this level life is not as difficult as it use to be.

Donna doesn't feel she has the confidence to be at that party this weekend. She feels over weight and not attractive enough. Finding your own special way to uplift her spirit could make her have a change of heart. Sometimes people are just not sure anymore and they really need your validation.

Many people commit suicide because life is just too difficult; too painful to continue. An improved self esteem could really turn things around. That's a switch from, I just can't to, now I can; a totally different feeling.

THE POWER OF BEING A LITTLE NICE

The simplest way to make someone feel important is to just be a little nice to that individual. It is important to remember that a person feels very important if you can just be a little nice to them. To you it's nothing but to the receiver it's a big deal. You literally change lives without even realizing it.

"Hey Tony how are you. I am glad to see you. I see you have lost the weight and you are in good shape. How are Liz and the kids? I knew you guys were inseparable. How is the job, have you had a promotion since? I know you have what it takes to be a good manager. Anyway it was nice seeing you again. Hope to see you soon". That alone will do it for someone's confidence. If this man had thoughts about giving up, that could be the turning point simply because you took the time off to acknowledge his presence.

Being a little nice to someone makes that person feel very important so there is no need to go out of your way to make them feel good. In fact this is where people begin to take advantage of you, mistaking your niceness for softness.

Weather we want to accept it or not we do need people in our lives. Sometimes we are running on empty, emotionally, where we begin to doubt our abilities and fear, worry and anxiety set in. Today, someone in their own unique way, made you feel good about your self and that's all you needed to get back on tract and regain your confidence.

This is one of the very important reasons for social gatherings like parties, dances sports clubs etc. We meet in those places like cars stopping at a gas station for a refill so we can continue our daily lives.

It is incredibly disappointing going to a party where most of the people don't seem to have the desire to interact with each other. This certain group of people that I am familiar with have baffled me for as long as I can remember. In almost every event, it's always about ten percent who seem to socialize and enjoy the moment.

I enjoy gatherings where every one is having fun, and every one is nice to each other at least for the moment. This is the reason why we come together; it is more than just eating drinking and dancing. I hope certain people can use this idea to relax their stuck up attitudes.

You can be a little nice to some one without giving him the wrong idea. That is no reason for you to exchange numbers if you don't want to. It is not a green light for me and my family and all my relatives to come and swim in your pool and we don't need to know each others personal affairs either.

In fact if I am a little nice to you and you happen to know some of my personal affairs that should not be out in public, you might just keep it buried and away from the ears of others.

This is the fastest way for a group of people to come together to accomplish a specific purpose; it could be the residents on one street or the people in an apartment building who are tired of a deteriorating life style to a basketball team that's had enough loses.

Family members and relatives could benefit a whole lot if they could just be a little nice to each other. This is the glue that binds people together and makes them stronger than ever. Try it and see for yourself.

WORDS SHAPE OUR LIVES

The words that you speak says what you think and what you think of constantly says what you believe and what you believe you are compelled to experience; you are subconsciously compelled to experience the things you believe in. It doesn't matter what you believe in weather it's good or bad, wrong or right. Once you get to that state where you truly believe something, it begins to manifest in your life.

A good example of a subconscious compulsion is a good or bad habit, an excessive compulsive behavior like washing your hands fifty times a day when there is no reason to or being addicted to some kind of chemical or drug. We need to be careful about the thoughts we entertain.

No matter what happened to you in the past, your life from this moment on depends on the way you think about yourself, about money, love, relationship and everything else. Many have had things said and done to them that play right into adulthood. They are literally hunted by these thoughts and mental images all their lives. The scary part is these thoughts continue to manifest as time goes on. That explains why many peoples' health, looks and financial status continue to deteriorate through out the years. We should decide what types of thoughts dominate our mind because we have the power to do so.

Repeat positive affirmations to yourself a few times daily until they take over the old thinking pattern. Repeating an affirmation three to five times a day works just fine for me. Some teachers suggest repeating them many times a day, but you should do what works best for you.

Don't expect overnight success or instant results especially where you have been experiencing wrong thoughts for many years. These old thoughts tend to give a challenge so you should just keep repeating your positive words until they dominate.

Very importantly, your choice of words will determine the effectiveness of the affirmation. You should never talk about what you don't want on a continuous basis, because that's exactly what you will get. Instead, use positive words in the present tense, example I am a good father to my kids. Yes, you may not be but if you keep that thought, you will, eventually. I am 'going' to finish my book in July 2003, is another way you can say it. Through trial and error you will find the right words that work for you.

When you have chosen the right word, phrase or sentence[s] you will know because it just feels right.

You can do everything except change your thinking about a problem and the change will only be temporary. For example people go on diet all the time only to fail a short time latter. You see the mind is way too powerful and it creates in your life whatever you say, think and believe about yourself. Lasting change only happens when your way of thinking changes and stays that way.

If you are the member of a family with a history of a certain illness, start repeating at least five times a day- every cell, tissue and organ in my body is completely healthy and in perfect order. Affirmations seem to work better when you include the Creator.

Genes are basically inherited memory. Your father had diabetes because of his life style. He ate too much sugar laden foods and did little to no exercise. The only reason you should get this problem is if you develop the same bad habits; not because of genes which basically says we are doomed to failure. Constant repetition of the above affirmation or whatever else suits you will eventually right your thinking.

Every year you get allergies like clock work. Why don't you change your thinking right now and see what happens the next time around?

Advertisers have a good understanding of how the mind works and their aim is to get you to buy whatever product is being advertised and they are getting better and better as time goes by. Like everything else, there is good and there certainly is bad, so it's up to you to decide weather or not you will be affected.

CAN WORDS HURT

Learn how to protect your self from the destructive words of others. You can slam the phone, walk out the room or turn off the television set. The words people direct at you can and will affect your mind if you don't stand guard.

This guy who has no goals and no aim is trying to convince you that you cannot make it as a musician, something you obviously love. Do you accept his words or do you interrupt what he is trying to get across to you? Know your true abilities, your history and that will act as a shield preventing negative people from getting to you.

You can use the negative words of others to motivate you. They say you are not a very smart guy and maybe they are right to a certain extent. Are you going to make enemies and be belligerent or are you going to read more and learn a few words from the dictionary on a daily basis. That could be your motivation to go back to school and earn some kind of diploma in a field of your choice. You can be guaranteed that you won't be hearing those hurtful words again.

If your wife calls you skinny, then work out. You will love it and she will love you even more. We benefit big time from these experiences.

The people who criticize too much never seem to realize how difficult they make it for themselves and their children. I know some people whose lives are so much harder because of the actions of their parents, and that's a fact. You send garbage out to others then garbage is what will return and unfortunately you are not the only one who gets hurt.

So many times we think that doing something wrong behind closed doors is ok because no one knows. Deliberately engaging in immoral behaviors can affect you seriously. Yes no one saw you did it so you think you can just go on with your life as normal. The problem is, the thoughts stay with you and your conscience wares you down day after day.

The thoughts of the wrongs that you have done to others or have been done to you can eat away at you like termites on a house, until such day when you decide to recondition you mind by changing your way of thinking.

Anna is pregnant and is concerned about the sex of her baby. I will be disappointed if it's not a girl, she said. After a few times, I had to remind her that she should be ready to accept whatever she gets. If it's a boy, I continued, and you keep expressing your dissatisfaction, by talking of how much you would rather have a girl, you may just end up seeing your boy behaving more and more feminine as he grows up. That's a scientific fact and I personally know of situations like this.

There is this girl I know very well who always says she would rather be a boy and she is acting more and more like it. One day I asked, did your mother want a boy instead of you? Yes she said. You see I know this family and sometimes people with three or more kids want to have a certain pattern like a boy then a girl followed by a boy and so on. In the case of Linda, her mother was expecting a boy.

Words are powerful and we have to be careful how we use them. Of course you don't want to be too careful you just want to mix it up a bit. If you are going to be negative as most people are, throw in just as many positives. For example, you are angry and say to your little boy, you know you are really stupid. I don't know why I am wasting my hard earned money sending you to school. Don't just stop there, you could mess the child's mind up. When you are relaxed say to the kid, in a serious way, I know you are capable of achieving whatever you want in life. I also know that you are smart enough and I have faith in you. That right there neutralizes the negative and averts future problems in his life.

CHOOSE YOUR FRIENDS

It is important to watch the people you associate with. People who engage in a life of crime are very slick. They can pull you into their web long before you know what's happening. This type of individual will try to pull you down to his level. The old saying misery loves company is true in this case. For example, Jim will not be too comfortable with the fact that he has to steal for a living while his brother or friend owns a legitimate business and makes a descent living. Trevor gets into your car with some drugs in his pocket. A little while latter you are pulled over by the cops, guess where he is going to hide the cocaine; right under your seat.

Sometimes the ones closest to you will technically and systematically destroy your self esteem and your self worth. They always make comments that come across as harmless but are slowly tearing you down like the waves on the coastline. We all have many people like that in our lives and should pay close attention.

I like being around people who can teach me something new. I am always willing to learn and grow in some way. Isn't that what life is all about?

Positive people, just being in their presence makes you feel energized; you feel relaxed and comfortable. Negative people on the other hand do quite the opposite.

I know from first hand experience that a person's energy really does rub of on you; that is, if you are too close for too long. The next time you come in contact with someone who has a very low self esteem, notice how quickly your energy is drained and how fast your mood changes and for how long it stays that way.

Sometimes we just know that we hate being around certain people; no real reason why we feel that way.

It's a great day today and you feel wonderful. You are playful, all smiles, then comes Dexter with all his doom and gloom that he just cannot seem to let go of. That atmosphere right there will replace your smile with a frown very quickly.

I really don't mind releasing a few people from my life every now and then. It's actually a very healthy habit because a long term relationship with some people can easily create a poisonous atmosphere. Where as her presence in you life was important, she is just not right for you anymore.

Have you wondered why you feel so light and comfortable since you and Jackson stopped being buddies? It seems like he weighted you down with some kind of heavy load. You certainly feel better off without him around.

WHY DO YOU ACT THE WAY YOU DO

It is important to understand the origin of your problem. A lady was explaining to me how she trembled everytime she ate anything except mashed potatoes. She learned why when she discussed the problem with her mother. When she was a child she hardly ate any other foods, and her mother would force her to eat by yelling, an action which made her nervous. With this understanding the condition slowly went away.

One of my relatives stole a lot as a kid. Nobody understood why because he had a descent home, living with his grand parents. There was enough to eat like any normal home, so what was his problem. It is said that when people steal compulsively, they are looking for attention. Kids who are virtually ignored by their parents tend to have that characteristic. This young man did not know his mother and was not acknowledged by his father.

Looking back, I remember a few other people who engaged in that type of behavior either never knew or were very much ignored by one or both parents.

If you can't find someone who can tell you a little about your past, maybe a hypnotherapist can help. The name may sound weird, but this is someone who can help you relax to the point where you are able to remember things that happened to you in the past; things that you have long forgotten. He is a therapist who incorporates hypnosis in his practice.

Though I have never met a hypnotherapist, I don't think I would have a problem visiting one. I would like to know why I flirt so much and at the same time be so picky.

I am sure everyone would like to know the origin of some of their behaviors and attitudes like, why is it at thirty nine you have never sat behind the steering wheel of a car or why are you so afraid of marriage or having children?

If you don't have that luxury, good old questions will do just fine. Ask your Self a specific question on a daily basis until the answer shows up. It will pup up when you least expect it, from the least expected people, under the least expected situations. You just need to pay attention.

WHATS IN A NAME

In one of our many discussions about the power of words, my friend Lee Sella made a few comments which I need to share with you. This is the tool that shapes our life, so we should pay attention to how we use it.

A Russian submarine named KURSK sank killing all on board. What does the word sound like to you? Is there any wonder why this tragedy happened? In New York there was a story of a young girl who shot the wife of her supposed lover. He had a speed boat named Double Trouble. A musician allegedly shot and killed another man in a night club, his nick name, murder.

The words we use and their meaning will manifest eventually.

I never liked my name until I became an adult. Understanding that words and names have meanings that tend to affect your life, I began appreciating it a little more. A few people tried explaining the meaning to me. Whether its correct or not I am quite comfortable with what I have heard.

My cousin was telling me that her coworker has a daughter named Stormy. Can you guess what her personality is like? Well in case you are wondering, her name and her attitude are synonymous.

TIRED OF YOUR ADDICTION?

According to the law of nature, everything begins in the mind and if you can imagine the things you want long enough you can have them. Now the point I am trying to make here is, if you are an alcoholic who wants to be clean, your mental image and the words you repeat will determine your success. You need to see yourself exactly the way you want to be which, is the exact opposite of your problem. If you say you are recovering, in the next twenty years you will still be a recovering addict. You get exactly what you say and think on a continuous basis.

Many of the people I know, who drink heavily tend to be shy or very quiet around others when sober. It's kind of annoying when this man who had so much to say at the party last night now barely wants to answer a yes or no question.

It's a very costly habit, drinking just for the purpose of socializing. That type of individual will very much likely become an alcoholic which for many has proven disastrous because your health, career, family and material possessions are at stake.

The easiest way to avoid this trap is to learn the art of conversation. You can start a conversation with a total stranger very easily by talking about something in common. For example you are standing at the bus stop, and you notice the bus is late, which is not unusual. Make a comment about that and maybe the person next to you will respond and a conversation could begin easily. Make comments about things you have some kind of interest in; things you have some knowledge of.

You have to look for an opportunity to start a conversation. If you do, you will realize there are many things to talk about. You have had all kind of experiences through out the years and the people around you have had similar experiences. So here is your chance to just make a statement and see where it goes. If no one responds to your comment, wait a while and put another one out there.

The stranger sitting next to you in a bar may try to start a discussion. If you are knowledgeable in this area add to it and see how much you can speak on the topic.

It's very easy for me to talk to anyone but I first had to learn this simple trick.

YOU GET WHAT YOU EXPECT

Our lives are shaped based on the way we see things. For example, I begin to sneeze and cough because I was out in the rain. I think to myself well I guess I am catching a cold. With that way of thinking I may just get sick. But If I think that my body is just fighting an infection, the cold might just go away.

You have asthma, do you have a breathing problem or is your body trying desperately to breathe normally. If you think it is the latter, then the question is what must I do to breathe naturally again? At this point you are not thinking about the asthma you are focusing on breathing right. This way of thinking makes you feel better.

You say you suffer with allergies and you expect it in the spring season. When spring arrives you refer to it as allergy season. When you sneeze, you tell the people close by that you are suffering from allergies. You look to the news today for the pollen count. On the train you easily recognize others suffering from the same problem. With that level of expectation, you won't be disappointed. Your allergies will show up right on time every year.

Don't think of the things you really don't want to experience. If you think constantly, of drugs like cocaine and how people use it, do you think that you might just try it one day and possibly get into the habit? Of course we all know the mind has a way of its own and thoughts pop up all the time beyond our control. That is normal but the problem starts when we entertain those thoughts that are not good for us; thoughts we really don't want taking shape in our lives.

THE GREAT STRESS RELIEVER

The understanding that everything happens for a reason, puts you in a relaxed state both physically and mentally. That should be your belief and the way to deal with even the simplest situations in your daily lives. For example, if you have just lost your car, it makes no sense dwelling on the lost, especially if there is no way of getting it back. You need to focus on getting another one as quickly as possible. While you are busy doing that try figuring out why you lost your car and what you need to do in the future to prevent that from happening again. At least you will learn some kind of valuable lesson. This way of thinking will keep you from wasting time experiencing the stress and tension you get by dwelling on your lost.

Everybody that we have met in this life time, we met for a good reason, weather we are aware of it or not. We are here on purpose. We all have a job to do and these people have only been helping us along that journey.

Look at an area of your life that you are happy about. Maybe you graduated from high school or college. Maybe you are an architect, a builder or an engineer. Maybe you raised well disciplined children or have your own home. What ever success you are proud of, take a look back down memory lane, and notice how everybody helped you get to that point. Both the good and so called bad people did what had to be done. The ones who gave you a hard time fueled your fire and those who supported you did so when you were too weak to carry on.

The questions you ask make you zero in on the right answers quickly. Your pastor, teacher, psychologist can help you find some of the answers you need but it is easy enough to do it on your own.

You can finally see why your parents are the way they are and suddenly you are not as angry as before. You didn't grow up with you father and looking at this guy now, with his views on life, his way of thinking, you understand why things happened the way they did and that puts you at ease. You should ask yourself questions knowing for a fact that you benefit from every experience.

When you know your talent you can have a good view of your life and a better understanding of how and why everything happened. You love construction more than anything else. Now you appreciate your father dragging you with him to work every single day of your summer holidays, or you are so happy that your music teacher was harder on you than anyone else.

There are times when an unpleasant memory will get to you, just return your focus to the benefits of the experience. That will help keep your sanity.

Understanding why you went through such difficult times in your life, you are now ready to free your Self completely by forgiving the people involved. Even if they knew what they were doing, there is no way they could have known why. So forgive them the best way you know how. Your mind is now free from the negativities which have been holding you back for so long.

BE YOUR SELF

Being yourself means going along with your feelings and doing the things you want to do as long as it's not harmful to others.

Many people go around giving the rest of the world the impression that they are prefect, always smiling always happy; nothing is ever wrong. They suppress all negative feelings, refusing to let them flow naturally. They will hold in the hurt and suppress the anger, then comes the inevitable explosion and the release of those emotions in the worst way. Learn to clear your mind by talking about what's bothering you and move on with your life.

Quiet people can be very explosive with their temper. You may not see it often but it can be frightening. This woman I know has the sweetest voice, then she explodes over something very insignificant and people two miles away can hear everything she says very clearly.

My step brother is a pretty quiet feller and though I have never seen him get angry I really don't want to see that.

The weird thing about situations like that is you can easily be fooled into believing that you are the cause of their intense anger. It is not a pleasant metaphor to explain my point but people like that are like a plastic garbage bag filled to capacity and the smallest break will cause the contents to spill all over the floor creating a mess. Every time I see someone blowing off fumes over something ridiculously insignificant, that's the best example I can think of.

DON'T LET MATERIAL THINGS CHANGE YOU

It's amazing how people change their personalities because of their material possessions. I am sure you have had a friend or associate who suddenly treats you differently because he now has a car a house or has gotten a new promotion at his job. I have seen this so many times its baffling.

I don't know what goes on in a person's mind, to suddenly be so different now that she has her own house. I guess she is seriously frightened by her accomplishments not realizing that she always had it in her.

I can go on the street right now and see a lady driving a nice car with the 'I don't want to be bothered' expression on her face. Definitely not everyone is like that but, way too many people are telling the world that they are not use to stuff like this.

You cannot allow yourself to be defined by the material things you possess. Let's say today I am living in an apartment and I have a small job and you have your own house and a higher paying job. That gives you the feeling that you are better than I am. You may consider me inferior to you. Tomorrow I am doing ten times better than you and all of a sudden you see me as superior to you. That is a total lack of understanding of Self.

WHAT'S YOUR VIEW ON AGEING

Louie seems very concerned about his advancing age. He is in his forties and sees those years coming fast. I said am in my thirties and thinks am getting old too. This gentleman thinks that it's down hill once you reach forty.

Every one who has reach thirty suddenly realizes that life is not that long and it seems very short if you keep giving attention to those numbers. On your thirtieth birthday, you are fresh out of your twenties and you realize that in nine years you will be forty. By the time you get use to the idea you are thirty five and that's the way life goes if you keep playing the number game. This my friend, makes one age rapidly.

You see I am not too concerned about that at all. What matters to me most is what I do with this limited time we all have been given here on this earth. My desire is to develop myself to the point where I can help make the world a better place.

First I am going to do that as a writer and motivational speaker. I will then use some of my wealth to further improve the lives of others. I have so many things I want to accomplish I just can't waste my time worrying about age.

There is a reason why my parents look younger than they are and that is their ages are never part of a conversation with anyone.

I almost never tell anyone my age because people are just too negative. In your twenties they tell you what you should not be doing anymore, in your early thirties they tell you a few more things you should not or cannot do simply because of your age. And the negativities toward you increase as time goes by. Given their way, people will finally get you to accept limitations due to your age that are absolutely baseless.

You are sixty and can run five miles everyday. To you this is a 'piece of cake', but the people around you bombard your mind so much, you finally begin to feel you are too old for this. They literally hypnotize you; yes we do this to each other all the time weather we are aware of it or not.

Many professional athletes are still healthy and strong enough to play a few more years, but are reminded of their ages and their limitations in practically every interview. They literally surrender from the constant pressures.

I know a few relatively young people who for whatever reason think they are old and they really do look much older than their actual ages. Two of my associates, one in her early twenties and one twenty seven both look forty plus though not at all times. In fact I have both their photographs and they don't look their ages at all; that's amazing.

LAUGHTER IS GOOD FOR YOU?

Humor neutralizes and minimizes the effects of negative emotions on our minds and bodies. It is truly a great medicine. Let's say you hate your coworker with a passion and this person happens to say something funny that made you laugh, suddenly, your feelings are not as strong anymore. Laughter cures anger, jealousy, resentment and other negativities.

As we all know these negatives emotions, held for too long, seriously affect ones health and overall success in life. This is why we all need to have a sense of humor.

In this high stressed world, is there any wonder why comedy is in such high demand? Sitcom stars and stand up comedians become rich making people laugh.

FOLLOW YOUR INSTINCTS

Intuition is your natural guide. It is your way of knowing when to run instead of walk. You know that you should not even attempt to start a relationship with this person even if she smiles most of the time and says all the right things. In the beginning you knew instinctively that she was the type who would take the house, prevent you from seeing the children and take most of your money, but you went ahead and got married to her anyway.

Your intuition is always right because it is God talking to you. You can't get around this fact. If you feel like doing something but it doesn't feel right then it's not good for you. If it feels right that means it's good.

You and your friends want to beat up some guys who have insulted you but you know there could be serious consequences; just reconsider that's all.

You broke up with your mate on Friday and your sentiments were not pretty. On Saturday the following day, you keep getting the feeling to call or go back to the house and the thoughts just won't go away. I am sure if you follow your deep feelings you won't regret.

Your reasoning is what gets you confused. That's why it is said that the initial feeling you get about a thing or person is usually right. You met Richard, your sister's boyfriend for the first time and you are not impressed. He acts like a gentleman, but you just have a bad feeling about this one. You can't really explain it, he just doesn't seem right. The mistake happens when you begin to focus on the things he says and the way he acts and you begin to disregard what you first felt. At this point your conscious reasoning takes over.

In this day and age of uncertainty you need to rely more and more on that still voice inside that only you can here. If you keep making a date with someone and things keep coming up that interrupt plans then maybe it is not meant to be.

This guy wants to go into business with you but plans never seem to go through, don't worry there is a good reason for this.

Many people have strict rules about their eating habits and will abide by those rules no matter what. You are not suppose to eat meat or any animal product but lately your body has been craving milk even if you have not had it in years. The question is how do you, or any other person knows that there isn't some type of chemical in milk that is absolutely important for your body right now? In this situation do you follow your rules or your instinct?

Sometimes your intuition could manifest as a freak accident. I was moving to a new apartment and the lady at the telephone company tried to convince me to change my number, a deal she would have made a percentage of because it costs more to have a new number. So I went ahead with her insistence. Just as she was about to complete the transaction the phone accidentally cut off. That was good because I didn't want to change my original number anyway.

You are about to eat some food and it accidentally falls on the floor. Would you think for a second that maybe it was tainted and you were not supposed to eat it?

LEARN TO RELAX

You need to learn how to relax both physically and mentally. Look at your shoulder right now, is it tense. If so, why do you think it is. Maybe you are trying too hard at what you do. Worrying about your bills, the children and a hundred other things can cause you to tense up.

Notice how tightly you hold the steering wheel sometimes; you are thinking to much, relax.

There are many different exercises that reduce mental and physical tension. Usually doing what you love makes you relax which means you can concentrate better and longer. You are relaxed when your mind is on one thing at least for a while.

Exercising is a stress reliever. This is one of the reasons why joggers just can't quit and when they do, it is missed.

Meditation and I mean the simple form, is an excellent way of staying centered. Virtually any kind of activity that makes you happy and captures you fullest attention is relaxing.

When you are too tense you are off balance so to speak. You are not your natural self. Think of something you do very well, in fact something you truly love. Now imagine yourself doing the same thing when you are too tense. Is it the same? Now, can you see your favorite basketball player in a game where he is unable to be himself because of too much tension? This will definitely be one of his worst games. How about a surgeon in the operating room unable to relax? Be glad its not you lying on that table.

I have noticed in professional sports especially basketball that some of the coaches tend to look very anxious, nervous or worried especially during the playoffs. Now that is not a very helpful attitude. Those feelings subliminally affect the team, taking away the edge it needs to win. That's one of the reasons why some teams always almost win.

However he does it, a coach should have total control of his emotion at least during playing time. He has to be mentally and physically relaxed. Being pumped up is one thing but having those other unhealthy emotions is totally unproductive and costly.

KEEP BUSY

There is a saying, keep moving or perish and evidence of that is every where. Do you know that if the shark stops moving it will drown? Well that's the nature of the life we are living and more of us should keep this in mind. You must keep going until you live this planet. If you can't do it physically then imagine it because the physical and the mental are one and the same.

It is really not a wise thing for a man to think of retirement as staying home and not lifting a finger. We all know this leads to an early grave.

I knew this gentleman who worked his entire life in Jamaica and came to spend his retirement in New York. I remember him telling me that he would never work for anyone again. He had no intention of holding another job. I must say he actually seemed very idle to me. You can guess what happened a short time later.

Retirement means giving up your job for the opportunity to do all the things that you never had the time to do earlier. So go play golf in the middle of the week, something most working people cannot afford to do. If you like photography, here is your chance.

Doing nothing all day once in a while is very healthy for you. Setting up a day where you do nothing all day is actually doing something; it's actually an activity. You have to notice your environment and see what could hinder your plan and do something about it. It's even better if you can have the house all to your self for most of the day. Let your family and friends understand that this day is exclusively yours where you don't have to do anything you don't want to, except in case of an emergency. So eat, watch television, read, listen to music, sleep, wake up, eat watch television, workout a little and sleep again. Its important to do whatever makes you comfortable.

BE READY FOR DIFFICULTIES

It is important to be prepared to face difficulties in life because they always show up. We are here to gain experience, to learn and develop into more mature intelligent beings. When you are faced with a tough challenge, you must understand that this is an opportunity to learn something new.

A boy becomes a man, a girl becomes a mature woman by accepting the situation or condition as it comes, picking out the good and moving on with life more prepared than before.

So many people allow themselves to be consumed by tragedy not realizing those are blessings in disguise. The term tragedy is relative because a breakup with my woman simply means something better is coming to me where as for Jane it means never trusting another man again no matter what.

Your fiance' backs out a few days before the wedding. It can be embarrassing but you should not be too hard on yourself because obviously this marriage is not supposed to happen.

It's a mistake to believe that because tough times make you stronger it's ok to actually go looking for trouble. What can happen is, according to your particular circumstance, you can end up doubling your trouble which could easily overwhelm you. Let's say, you are destined to become a surgeon and your motivation has to come from living with a sick mother throughout your childhood, now that's difficult enough for a young person to live with. What if you allow your self to be influenced by your peers and get involved in some serious crimes causing you to go to jail for a very long time? These two situations could be too much, even for the strong.

In many cases, the difficulty you experience is just a test to prove that you really want the things you say you want. We all hear time and time again of those who reach the top in their chosen fields and the tough times they had to overcome. Many of us who desire the same things would have given up after two failed attempts. When you get to the point where you have seen the tough road ahead, have gone through many disappointments and have made up your mind that you are going to get there no matter what, you shall have what ever it is you are looking for.

TOUGH TIMES KIDS FACE

Often in a divorce or break up these little people have to endure too much pain at the hands of the adults involved, who are in many cases very immature themselves. The kids are often the last to understand what's really going on and are often asked to take sides however ridiculous it may seem. Yes this man wants his seven year old girl to understand that her mother is bad and wants to destroy her perfect world.

Two adults fighting verbally or physically seem like a real war to a child and can be a highly traumatic experience.

Someone told me that in his country it is quite normal for the people of a community to chase an accused thief and beat him to death. For a very young child, this is not a good experience. They could spend the rest of their lives being defensive. Remember when you were little what would your imagination be like if you herd that a man was just killed a few blocks from your house, for doing something bad? That could definitely affect you state of mind for a long time to come.

Adults tend to make the mistake of feeling that they are far superior to the children. That they should only obey orders and do as told and should speak only when spoken to. So most times the kid's thoughts, feelings and problems go unheard or unacknowledged. Do you remember what it felt like when your 'world' wasn't right and this big old dictator they call a parent, wouldn't give you the time of day to express your self? Everybody has issues, but the child's is usually considered insignificant.

I remember being a kid like it was yesterday, and to me, many of the adults around me were just plain old bullies. They had all the power and you had none and boy, that used to 'piss' me off. I saw myself as a regular person, intelligent with a good understanding of every thing around me and there were these people, like most adults, acting like I were their subject. They expect you to turn left or right, walk straight backwards or hop on one leg so to speak, if you were told to. That's one of the reasons young people grow up with such bad temper.

Adults are always automatically right no matter what and this can be incredibly frustrating to a young person. It is surprising even when you have grown up these people still intend to keep up the habit.

There comes the part, from the child's perspective, in many cases is absolutely ridiculous. She reacts to a situation which is seriously affecting her state of mind and instead of seeing that as a sign of trouble, she is disciplined. You are basically taught to accept things as they are and keep your mouth shut.

Don't let the kids suppress all those negative feelings and emotions; that can be disastrous. Try and get to their level every once in a while and have a conversation. You really want to know what's going on in you child's life so ask questions like the curious kid next door. Allow them to have the floor. Just listen for once and maybe you will learn something new today.

TEENAGERS

If you show your teens that you trust them to do the right things, they more than likely will meet your expectation. These people are usually very intelligent, so they don't need a lecture from you every day. What they need mainly, is to be reminded to stay forever focused on what's important.

Weather they show you or not you need to stay in touch; they expect you to. No matter how busy you are you can always find five minutes to have a little discussion with you children. That makes them feel important and builds their self esteem and confidence. Any kid would be flattered when a parent takes time off her busy schedule and dedicate a few moments entirely to him.

Make them feel comfortable enough to answer your questions about school, about life, relationships, their likes and dislikes and views about what's going on around them.

The more informed you are about your adolescents the more you are able to relax and give them more control of their lives. We all know that the toughest job any one can do is to control young people who are about to turn into adults. They are filled with energy and the best you can hope for is to help guide not suppress and control these energies.

They are going to do exactly what you don't want them to do so be careful with the negatives. Parents who fight desperately to keep their girls away from boys always seem to fail. There is a saying that you can never get enough of what you don't want. So if you keep your attention on chasing the boys away, you will get the exact opposite.

There is a popular misconception that the girls who hang around many boys tend to be promiscuous. Contrary to those beliefs these tend to have the most control when dealing with males and have way less sex than others are lead to believe. Many a men have been surprised to find out that the girl who everyone thought spreads herself around isn't so at all.

If you keep showing your child that you don't trust him to handle things on his own, you are doing much harm. You are basically reminding him on a daily basis that he is not strong enough, not intelligent enough, or good enough and that's debilitating. Instead of building self confidence he loses trust in his abilities.

'TWO LEFT HANDS'

I don't know what this means in other cultures but I grew up knowing that it is used to describe a person who just cannot seem to get almost any thing right. Instantly, you know this is the result of over critical or over cautious adults. What grownups say to the young carries a lot of weight and way too many people get hurt that way.

On any given day listen to any adult talking to a child and in five minutes you will hear, fifty can'ts, don,ts, should nots, that's bad and many more.

A man who finds it hard changing a simple light bulb, and a woman who cannot seem to fry the egg properly, might be victims of too much criticism from people in power.

It is said that one of the reason people stutter is because of too much criticism experienced in childhood. We do whatever we can to avoid pain and hurt, so if speaking gets us in trouble then we will find a way to shut down. We become very shy, quiet or lose our ability use words effectively.

WE ARE NATURAL BORN WINNERS

We tend to always have the things that we absolutely must have. Find the poorest most negative person, and you will find that he always has some form of food, clothing and shelter because they are absolutely important to him. Anytime you get to the point where you cannot imagine, or you refuse to imagine yourself without something because of its importance to you, you will have it.

The man who absolutely must have a car will always be behind a steering wheel where as the man who doesn't think that way may or may not have one.

Our fears and doubts are the killers of our success. This is the reason why it is said that man is his own worst enemy. They are the main obstacles preventing us from accomplishing our desires. We always flourish in areas where we are not experiencing these two mental blocks.

I have the need to repeat, that we can never lose. Your wife left you and a good woman she is. You lost her but you learned that you need to grow up emotionally. You need to have control of your emotions. Maybe she got tired of you because you are too stingy. Now you know that this attitude is unhealthy, it is a lack of confidence in Self; a poverty mentality.

It's too late now, but you learn that you cannot use toys to replace quality time with your kids. These experiences make you wiser.

In most cases the lessons are a hundred times more valuable than the material things lost. For example, you own a business worth fifty thousand, but because of mismanagement and bad attitude you lost everything. Taken in a positive way, this fifty thousand dollar lesson prepares you for unlimited success the next time around.

I know you probably have read the autobiography of at least one great person in your lifetime and was impressed. What you may not have realized is the best one you will ever hear is your own life story and that's the truth. If you become more observant and pay attention to the way your life is unfolding, understanding that everything is happening for a reason and there is good in every situation you experience, you will become the most interesting person you have ever met.

About the Author

A former teacher of his native Dominica, Joshua Magloire has lived in the US for fourteen (14) years. He is the author of STOP FEAR and START Living: Getting into the State of Flow.

He is intensly passionate about learning and understanding human nature.